GOOSEY'S GOOD NEWS

WRITTEN BY: KENDALL WHITE

ILLUSTRATED BY: BRYCE WHITE

ISBN: 979-8-9948405-1-1

DEDICATION

To our own Goosey and Bear – your beautiful desire to share the Good News is the reason this book exists.

DEEP IN PINECONE FOREST, GOOSEY THE GOOSE FLAPPED HER WINGS EXCITEDLY.

"FRIENDS," SHE HONKED, "I HAVE THE MOST WONDERFUL NEWS IN THE WHOLE WORLD!"

"BUT BEFORE I TELL IT, I ALWAYS ASK, 'MAY I TELL YOU ABOUT JESUS?'"

"SOME FRIENDS SAY YES. SOME SAY NOT YET. AND THAT'S OKAY."

"WHEN SOMEONE ISN'T READY, WE JUST KEEP BEING KIND AND KEEP PRAYING."

THE BEAR AND FOX SCOOTED CLOSER.
"GOOSEY... WHO IS JESUS?"

MORE ANIMALS JOINED. GOOSEY SMILED. "SOME SAY HE WAS A GREAT TEACHER. SOME SAY HE WAS THE SON OF GOD."

"BUT THE BIBLE TELLS US THE
TRUTH–JESUS IS GOD."

"LONG AGO, THE FIRST PEOPLE DISOBEYED GOD. THAT DISOBEDIENCE WAS CALLED SIN."

"SIN SEPARATED PEOPLE FROM GOD, AND THAT MADE GOD SAD.

"BUT GOD ALREADY HAD A RESCUE PLAN."

"HE CAME TO EARTH AS JESUS! JESUS TAUGHT PEOPLE, HEALED THE SICK, AND FORGAVE SINS."

"MANY PEOPLE FOLLOWED HIM... BUT SOME DIDN'T BELIEVE."

"THEY WERE JEALOUS AND ANGRY,
AND THEY DECIDED TO HURT HIM."

"IT SOUNDS SCARY, BUT JESUS WASN'T AFRAID. HE CAME TO GIVE HIS LIFE FOR US."

"THEY PUT JESUS ON A CROSS. THEY DIDN'T KNOW IT WAS PART OF GOD'S PLAN."

"JESUS GAVE HIS LIFE TO PAY FOR EVERY SIN."

"AND AFTER THREE DAYS...
HE ROSE AGAIN! A MIRACLE!"

"HE DEFEATED SIN, DEATH, AND THE GRAVE SO WE CAN BE FORGIVEN."

THE CHIPMUNKS GASPED. "SO HOW DO WE GET SAVED?"

"I'M GLAD YOU ASKED!" GOOSEY HONKED."
"JESUS PROMISED A SPECIAL GIFT- THE HOLY SPIRIT."

"HIS FOLLOWERS WAITED AND PRAYED. THEN CAME THE FESTIVAL CALLED PENTECOST."

"A MIGHTY RUSHING WIND FILLED THE ROOM! GOD'S SPIRIT CAME!"

"THEY BEGAN SPEAKING IN LANGUAGES THEY HAD NEVER LEARNED."
"IT WAS A MIRACLE!"

"PETER TOLD
THE CROWD,
'THIS IS WHAT
GOD PROMISED
LONG AGO!'"

"THE PEOPLE ASKED, 'WHAT MUST WE DO TO BE SAVED?'"

"PETER SAID, 'REPENT, BE BAPTIZED IN JESUS' NAME, AND YOU WILL RECEIVE THE HOLY SPIRIT.'"

GOOSEY EXPLAINED:
"REPENT—TELL GOD
YOU'RE SORRY AND
CHOOSE TO DO
WHAT'S RIGHT."

"BE BAPTIZED IN JESUS' NAME-HE WASHES YOUR SINS AWAY."

"GOD FILLS YOUR HEART, AND YOU SPEAK IN A NEW LANGUAGE AS A SIGN."
"THAT'S RECEIVING THE HOLY SPIRIT!"

"AND THAT'S
JUST THE
BEGINNING!"
GOOSEY HONKED.
"YOU CAN LIVE FOR
JESUS
EVERY
DAY...

AND SHARE HIS LOVE
WITH OTHERS TOO."

SEE YOU NEXT TIME!

ABOUT THE AUTHOR

Kendall and Bryce serve together in children's ministries, where their passion is helping kids discover biblical truth, experience the presence of God, and grow in confidence and purpose. Their work reflects a shared commitment to creating environments where children feel seen, valued, and empowered to live out their faith. Through teaching, organizing, and hands-on ministry, they strive to support families and churches in raising the next generation of disciples.

www.ingramcontent.com/pod-product-compliance
Lightning Source LLC
LaVergne TN
LVHW070159110826
845147LV00002B/443

* 9 7 9 8 9 9 4 8 4 0 5 1 1 *